Families

Aunts and Uncles

Revised Edition

Rebecca Rissman

Heinemann Library
Chicago, Illinois

www.capstonepub.com
Visit our website to find out more information about Heinemann-Raintree books.

To order:
Phone 800-747-4992
Visit www.capstonepub.com to browse our catalog and order online.

© 2011, 2021 Heinemann Library
an imprint of Capstone Global Library, LLC
Chicago, Illinois

All rights reserved. No part of this publication may be reproduced or transmitted in any form or by any means, electronic or mechanical, including photocopying, recording, taping, or any information storage and retrieval system, without permission in writing from the publisher.

Edited by Rebecca Rissman and Catherine Veitch
Designed by Ryan Frieson
Picture research by Tracy Cummins
Originated by Capstone Global Library Ltd

Library of Congress Cataloging-in-Publication Data is available on the Library of Congress website.
ISBN 9781484668290 (pb)

Acknowledgments
We would like to thank the following for permission to reproduce photographs: Alamy: ONOKY - Photononstop, 19; Getty Images: Betsie Van der Meer, 9, David Sacks, 14, Fuse, 16, Henrik Sorensen, 4, Jon Feingersh Photography Inc, 15, JR Carvey/Streetfly Studio, 11, 23 top, Larry Williams, back cover, 12, 23 bottom, Michael H, 21, Rick Gomez, 17, Ronnie Kaufman, cover, Thomas Barwick, 20, 23 top middle, Yellow Dog Productions, 18; iStockphoto: Diane Labombarbe, 22, TriggerPhoto, 8; Shutterstock: Drazen Zigic, 6, feeling lucky, 5, 23 bottom middle, Kacso Sandor, 7, Monkey Business Images, 10, Picsfive, 13

We would like to thank Anne Pezalla and Nancy Harris for their invaluable help in the preparation of this book.

Every effort has been made to contact copyright holders of any material reproduced in this book. Any omissions will be rectified in subsequent printings if notice is given to the publisher.

Printed in the United States 6012

Contents

What Is a Family? 4
What Are Families Like? 8
Who Are Aunts and Uncles? 10
Different Aunts and Uncles 14
Family Tree 22
Picture Glossary. 23
Index 24

What Is a Family?

A family is a group of different people.

People in a family are called family members.

Family members care for one another.

All families are different.
All families are special.

What Are Families Like?

Families can be big or small.

Families enjoy doing things together.

Who Are Aunts and Uncles?

Some families have aunts and uncles.

Aunts and uncles are your parents' sisters and brothers.

Your parent's sister is your aunt.
Your parent's brother is your uncle.

Some families call special friends aunts and uncles.

Different Aunts and Uncles

Some families have many aunts and uncles.

Some families have few aunts and uncles. Some families have none.

Some people's aunts and uncles live with them.

Some people's aunts and uncles live far away.

Some aunts and uncles are young.
Some aunts and uncles are old.

Some aunts and uncles have children of their own.

If your aunts and uncles have children, they are your cousins.

Do you have aunts and uncles?

Family Tree

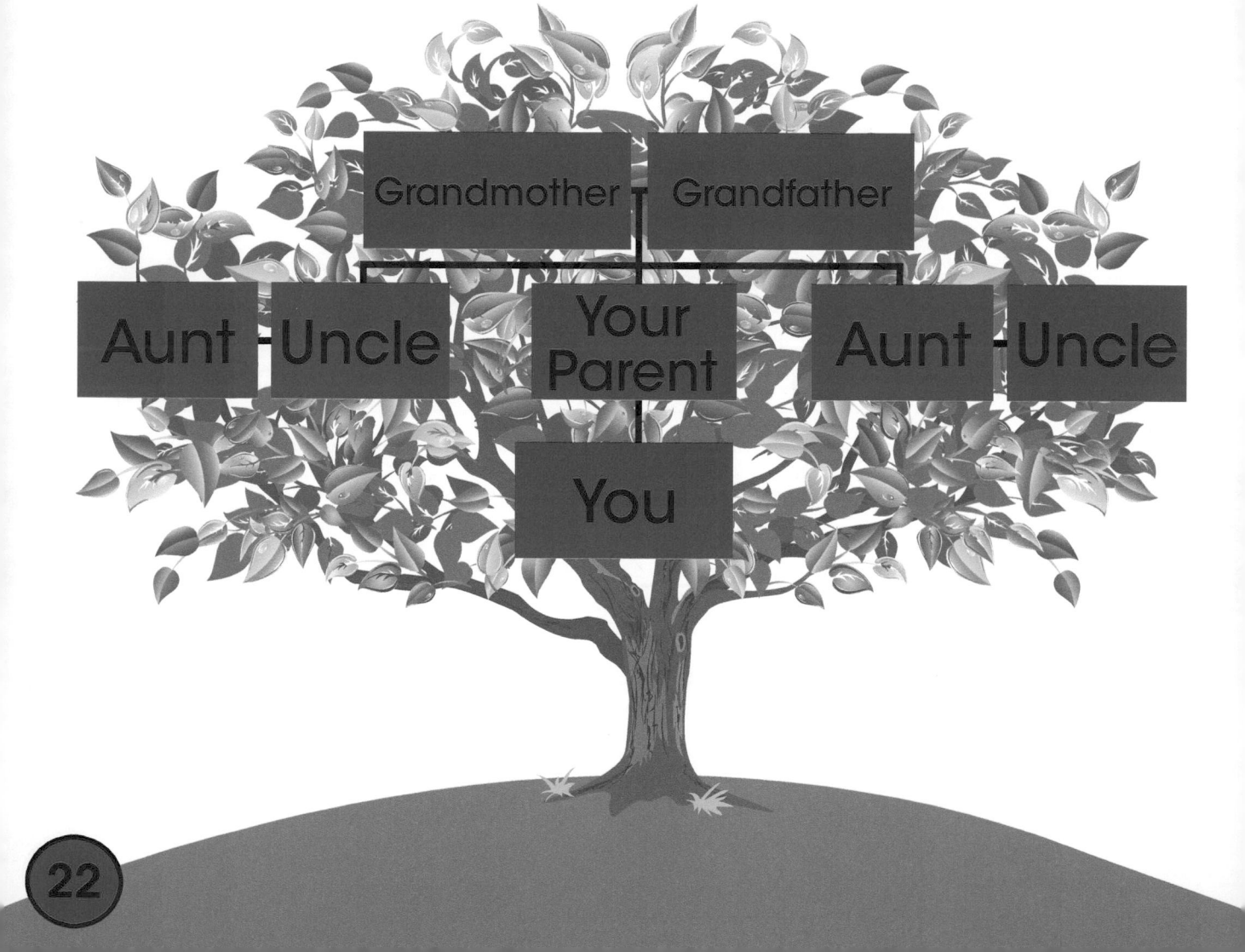
Grandmother
Grandfather
Aunt
Uncle
Your Parent
Aunt
Uncle
You

Picture Glossary

aunt a parent's sister

cousin child of an aunt or uncle

member person who belongs to a group

uncle a parent's brother

Index

aunt 10, 11, 12, 13, 14, 15, 16, 17, 18, 19, 21, 22
cousin 20
parent 11, 12, 22
uncle 10, 11, 12, 13, 14, 15, 16, 17, 18, 19, 20, 21, 22

Note to Parents and Teachers

Before Reading

Ask children to name different people who can be in a family (e.g., parents, grandparents, brothers, sisters, cousins). Record their answers in a list on the board. Then ask children if they know who aunts and uncles are, and how they can be related to their families. Explain that aunts and uncles are usually the sisters and brothers of parents.

After Reading

After reviewing the family tree on page 22, encourage children to draw their own family tree. If they have aunts and uncles, help the children to include them on their family tree.